It's fun to draw Ponies and Horses

Mark Bergin

Sky Pony Press
New York

Mark Bergin was born in Hastings, England. He has illustrated an award-winning series and written over twenty books. He has done many book designs, layouts, and storyboards in many styles including cartoon for numerous books, posters, and advertisements. He lives in Bexhill-on-Sea with his wife and three children.

HOW TO USE THIS BOOK:

Start by following the numbered splats on the left-hand page. These steps will ask you to add some lines to your drawing. The new lines are always drawn in red so you can see how the drawing builds from step to step. Read the "You can do it!" splats to learn about drawing and shading techniques you can use.

Sky Pony Press books may be purchased in bulk at special discounts for sales promotion, corporate gifts, fund-raising, or educational purposes. Special editions can also be created to specifications. For details, contact the Special Sales Department, Sky Pony Press, 307 West 36th Street, 11th Floor, New York, NY 10018 or info@skyhorsepublishing.com.

Sky Pony® is a registered trademark of Skyhorse Publishing, Inc.®, a Delaware corporation.

Visit our website at www.skyponypress.com.

10 9 8 7 6 5 4 3 2

Manufactured in China, November 2019
This product conforms to CPSIA 2008

Library of Congress Cataloging-in-Publication Data

Bergin, Mark, 1961-
It's fun to draw ponies and horses / Mark Bergin.
pages cm
Summary: "Drawing a horse just standing alone on the page is tricky enough, but with the help of this book you'll not only be able to draw as many as you like, but you'll master the art of horses in action--horses rearing up, kicking out, pulling a plow, running through a field, and so much more"-- Provided by publisher.
ISBN 978-1-63220-415-8 (paperback)
1. Horses in art--Juvenile literature. 2. Drawing--Technique--Juvenile literature. I. Title.
NC783.8.H65B47 2015
743.6'596655--dc23
2015007066

Cover illustration credit Mark Bergin

Contents

Rearing horse

1 Start by drawing a bean shape for the body.

2 Draw in the legs and hooves.

splat-a-fact
A male horse is called a stallion.

you can do it!
Use a felt-tip marker for the lines, then add color using crayons.

3 Draw in the head, mouth, neck, and tail.

4 Draw in the ears and mane. Add dots for the eye and nostrils.

4

5

Rodeo horse

1 Start by drawing the body.

Splat-a-fact

Rodeos test cowboys' riding skills to the limit.

2 Draw in the legs and hooves.

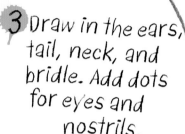

3 Draw in the ears, tail, neck, and bridle. Add dots for eyes and nostrils.

you can do it!

Use a felt-tip marker for the lines and add colored ink washes.

4 Draw in the saddle. Add the cowboy's legs and arm.

5 Complete the cowboy holding on to the reins.

Shire horse

1 Start by drawing a bean shape for the body.

2 Draw in four legs.

3 Draw in the head, ears, neck, and tail. Add the harness.

Splat-a-fact

Shire horses are one of the largest horse breeds.

4 Draw in the face and bridle details. Add a plow and a line for the field.

You can do it!

Use felt-tip marker for the lines. Color in with colored crayons and blend with your fingers.

5 Draw in the farmer.

Horse's head

1 Start by cutting out the shape of the head and neck. Glue down.

splat-a-fact
Horses love to eat hay.

2 Cut out the ears and glue down. Draw in the eyes, nostrils, and mouth.

you can do it!
Cut out the shapes from colored paper and glue in place. Use a felt-tip marker for details.

10

3 Cut out the brown mane and white nose patch. Glue down.

Galloping horse

1 Start with a bean shape for the body.

2 Draw in the head, neck, and tail.

you can do it!
Use a felt-tip marker for the lines. Use crayons for detail, then paint on top—the wax will act as a resistant.

splat-a-fact
Horses are herbivores (plant eaters).

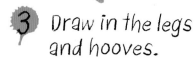

3 Draw in the legs and hooves.

4 Add the markings, mane, eye, nostril, and mouth.

Dressage

1 Start by drawing a bean shape for the body.

you can do it!

Use a black felt-tip marker for the lines. Color in with colored felt-tip markers.

2 Draw in the legs and hooves. Add a line for the ground.

3 Draw in the blanket, tail, and head. Add the bridle and a dot for the eye.

4 Draw in the ear and mane. Add a rider, saddle, and the reins.

15

Shetland pony

1 Start by drawing a bean shape for the body.

2 Draw in the legs and hooves.

you can do it!
Use a felt-tip marker for the lines and add color using colored oil pastels.

splat-a-fact
Shetland ponies are small and are often ridden by children.

3 Add a tail and grass.

4 Draw in the head details and long mane.

16

Racing horse

1 Start by drawing a bean shape for the body.

2 Draw in the legs and hooves.

You can do it!
Use a felt-tip marker for the lines and add color using chalk pastels.

3 Draw in the head and blinker hood. Add the neck, saddle, blanket, and tail.

4 Draw in the jockey holding on to the reins.

Pony family

1 Start by drawing two overlapping bean shapes.

2 Draw in the ponies' legs and hooves. Add the ground line.

you can do it!

Draw the lines with a felt-tip marker and use torn tissue paper for color.

Splat-a-fact

Foals learn to stand within an hour of being born.

3 Draw in two heads and necks.

4 Add the face details, ears, manes, and tails.

20

Stable

1 Start with a bean shape for the body.

you can do it!
Use a felt-tip marker for the lines and add highlights with white crayon. Add colored ink washes.

2 Draw in the legs and hooves.

3 Draw in the head and neck.

Splat-a-fact
Stables keep horses warm at night.

4 Add the face, ears, mane, and tail.

22

Military horse

1 Start with a bean shape for the body.

2 Draw in the legs and hooves.

Splat-a-fact
Horses have been used in warfare for over 5,000 years.

3 Draw in the head, neck, and tail. Add the face and ears, then the bridle and saddle.

4 Draw in the soldier holding his sword.

24

Rolling horse

1 Start with a bean shape for the body.

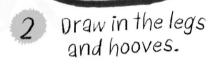

2 Draw in the legs and hooves.

splat-a-fact

Sometimes horses roll on the ground to stretch their muscles.

you can do it!

Use a felt-tip marker for the lines and then add color with watercolor paints. Dab on more color with a sponge for added texture.

3 Draw in the neck and head.

4 Draw in the face details and ears. Add the mane and tail.

Polo horse

1 Start by drawing a bean shape for the body.

2 Draw in the legs and hooves.

you can do it!
Use a felt-tip markers for the lines. Use colored pencils to color in. Place paper on a bumpy surface to add texture.

splat-a-fact
A polo team has four players.

3 Draw in the head, face, and bridle. Add the tail and saddle.

4 Draw in the polo player with a stick and ball.

Show jumping

1 Start with a bean shape for the body.

2 Draw in the legs and hooves. Add a tail.

you can do it!

Use felt-tip marker for the lines and add scribble textures with crayon. Paint over with a watercolor wash.

Splat-a-fact

A show jumping course consists of different obstacles to jump over.

3 Draw in the head, neck, bridle, and saddle blanket.

4 Draw in the rider holding the reins. Add the saddle.

Index